A COMMERCIAL CLIENT'S GUIDE TO ENGAGING AN ARCHITECT

RIBA Publishing

© RIBA Publishing, 2017

Published by RIBA Publishing, part of RIBA Enterprises Ltd, The Old Post Office,
St Nicholas Street, Newcastle upon Tyne, NE1 1RH

ISBN 978-1-85946-805-0

The right of Nigel Ostime to be identified as the Author of this Work has been
asserted in accordance with the Copyright, Designs and Patents Act 1988
sections 77 and 78.

British Library Cataloguing-in-Publication Data
A catalogue record for this book is available from the British Library.

Commissioning Editor: Elizabeth Webster
Project Editor: Daniel Culver
Production: Philip Handley
Designed by Kneath Associates
Typeset by Full Point Creative Media Ltd
Printed and bound by Page Bros, Norwich, UK

www.ribaenterprises.com

CONTENTS

	Introduction	ii
	Foreword	iii
	Preface	iv
	Acknowledgements	vi
	About the author	vii
01	Do I need an architect?	01
02	Selecting an architect	05
03	How do architects charge their fees and how much are they?	08
04	Appointing an architect – agreeing the terms and the scope of work	12
	Case Study 1: The Toffee Factory	18
05	Engaging other consultants	20
06	Project process – key stages in developing the building	24
07	Construction (Design and Management) Regulations 2015	34
08	Relevant legislation	38
	Case Study 2: The Avenue	42
09	RIBA Chartered Practices	44
10	ARB and RIBA codes of conduct	46
11	RIBA Find an Architect	48
12	RIBA Competitions	49
13	RIBA Client Advisers	52
14	Managing disputes	53
15	Client checklist of actions with key milestones and watch points	55
	Further reading	58
	Glossary	59
	Image Credits	61

INTRODUCTION

The aims of this book are to:

— Improve project outcomes through a considered process of selection of the architect by the client

— Inform clients of the value architects can bring to their projects

— Provide best practice advice on, and a full understanding of, the legal requirements of the appointment process

— Provide clients with an explanation of the project process.

This guide can be used by architects to explain the project process to their clients and the role of the architect within that process. Architects may find it helpful to give a copy to their clients at the commencement of a project.

FOREWORD

This book is an addition to the wealth of material which the Royal Institute of British Architects (RIBA) has developed to strengthen the client–architect relationship and improve project outcomes. The Institute has for some time now focused on clients as one of its core programmes through the 'RIBA for Clients' initiative, led by the Client Liaison Group, and that continues under my presidency.

The RIBA aims to champion better buildings, communities and the environment through architecture and our members. One way the institute can do this is by providing clients with the means to select the most appropriate architect for their project and inform them of the sort of questions they should be asking and what to expect during the project process.

This easily digestible but comprehensive guide provides the key information needed to engage the most appropriate architect for your project and to get the most value from the relationship. Take a few hours to read it and absorb the recommendations before you commence your project – it will be the most valuable time you spend on it.

Ben Derbyshire
RIBA President

PREFACE

I was pleased to be asked to update this publication because it ties in with the work of the RIBA Client Liaison Group that I have chaired since its inception in 2013. The group has conducted sector-focused roundtables, one-to-one filmed interviews and an online client satisfaction survey – the first of its kind in the industry, as well as other client-focused initiatives. Having more than 2,000 clients in our client database enabled us to develop and share unique insight into what it is that clients want from their architects. That data has been fed into this Client Guide and will help to improve outcomes on all projects in all sectors.

There is considerable detail in the results of the survey which can be downloaded free of charge, along with a wealth of other information by searching 'client survey' at **www.architecture.com**.

We found that architects' designs are generally considered to be of high quality and meet (or exceed) the requirements of the brief. The process of managing projects has room for improvement and there is advice in this guide to achieve that. A significant but unsurprising finding was that qualified architects perform better than non-qualified designers on all counts.

The architectural profession has rightly been praised for turning the mirror on itself through the survey, showing maturity and a desire to achieve continuous improvement, and I hope this guide will continue in that vein and help us, through good client–architect dialogue, to achieve better outcomes on all projects.

With increasing use of the internet and comparison websites it is easier than ever to select the provider with the lowest price. Consumers always have to be careful that they are comparing like with like, however, and this is particularly the case with professional services. Clients must take care in their selection processes, because the choice of architect will have a profound effect on the outcome of the project. Cost is always an important factor but value and the level of service being provided must also be considered, especially where the investment has a long-term impact, as is the case when developing the built environment – be it a major infrastructure project or a workplace refurbishment.

Nigel Ostime

ACKNOWLEDGEMENTS

The author would like to thank Linda Stevens, Head of Client Services at the RIBA, whose drive and enthusiasm has been key to the Client Liaison Group since its inception and who has been an enormous help in producing this book. He would also like to thank Rob Earl, Client Services Manager at the RIBA, and the members of the Client Liaison Group, past and present, for their enthusiasm and ideas, and in particular Matt Thompson who has produced insightful articles disseminating our findings as well as the text for the case studies in this book. Thank you also to the architects and clients of the case studies. They have illuminated the narrative and lent it a real-life perspective. Finally, thanks to Paul Bussey and Peter Waxman for sharpening the chapter on CDM.

ABOUT THE AUTHOR

Nigel Ostime is an architect and Project Delivery Director at Hawkins\ Brown, a practice regarded for its people-focused approach and strong design ethos.

Nigel has wide experience in the design and delivery of complex projects in sectors as diverse as aviation, infrastructure, commercial offices, high-end residential, retail, town centre mixed-use and industrial/ distribution buildings. He has delivered planning permissions on sensitive sites, both urban and rural, and has expertise in the management and coordination of multidisciplinary consultant teams through all project stages.

He is an active member of the RIBA, currently being a member of the Practice and Profession Committee and chair of the Client Liaison Group, which provides an interface between the institute and client bodies. He also sits on the RIBA Health and Safety steering group and set up the Future Leaders initiative, an education programme for business-focused, post-Part 3 skills for architects. He has been a member of the RIBA Plan of Work review group and the RIBA Professional Services Contract review group.

He has edited the last two editions of the *RIBA Job Book* (2008 and 2013) and the *Handbook of Practice Management* (2009 and 2013), and is author of the *Small Projects Handbook* (2014). He has developed two toolkits for RIBA members, one for quality management and the other for the briefing/evaluation process.

He lectures at Manchester, Westminster and The Bartlett schools of architecture and is a regular speaker at architecture and construction industry conferences on a range of topics.

01

DO I NEED AN ARCHITECT?

Kevin McCloud,
developer and
TV presenter,
Grand Designs

"

A good architect actually pays for themselves – more than once. You will reap the reward and the building will be hugely better and deliver much better value for it. "

Getting value out of the development process is a challenge, particularly if you are an owner-occupier or a first-time or fairly new developer. Appointing an architect from an early stage is central to optimising your property asset and creating value.

Architects apply impartial and creative thinking whether you are planning a new building, or adapting or expanding an existing property. They are problem-solvers and can develop solutions and efficiencies before and during construction.

Architects will work to understand your needs and support your strategic decision-making. From an early stage your architect can assess the site, set out the options, carry out feasibility studies and help you develop the strategic brief into the project brief.

They will assess the best ways to achieve your aspirations and will present options to you and your stakeholders, enabling you to decide on the best route forward. An architect will work to understand your business and ensure that you maximise your investment.

Architects add value, whether it comes from designing a product that is attractive to the market, changing use, improving functionality, increasing capacity or making a scheme more buildable. They will develop solutions and propose ways to reduce cost.

Architects can set up and lead the design team, manage the consultation and planning application processes and help to select the most appropriate procurement process and the contractor. They can also perform post-occupancy evaluation (POE) should this be required.

A survey conducted by the *Architect's Journal* a few years ago found that what architects do is largely a mystery to the general public: 72 per cent of people did not know that architects apply for planning permission; 86 per cent didn't know that architects select, negotiate with and manage contractors; and quite astonishingly 15 per cent did not know that architects design buildings! So an important first step in answering the question 'Do I need an architect?' is to cover the basics. This guide will do that as well as explaining how and where architects can add value and actually save cost.

Cost is always an issue and, as purchasers of goods and services, our instinct is to pay the lowest price we find available in the market. But alongside cost it is important to also consider value. This is particularly the case with such long-term investments as property development, alteration and refurbishment.

An architect will be able to advise not just on how to optimise the capital construction cost, but also on minimising cost in use. This is important because the cost of maintaining and operating buildings through their life can be more than the construction cost.

Building projects are complicated and as a consequence carry risk, and managing the risk is a value-adding exercise. They also obviously have to be done correctly first time. One of the great architects of the 20th century, Frank Lloyd Wright, famously said: 'A doctor can bury his mistakes but an architect can only advise his clients to plant vines'. Happily, the 2016 RIBA Working with Architects client satisfaction survey found that architects' design skills and ability to interpret and develop the brief are highly rated (78 per cent of clients were very or fairly satisfied with the aesthetic qualities of the project and 69 per cent of clients were very or fairly satisfied with the architect's ability to develop and interpret the brief). And with the ubiquitous rise of the use of 3D computer programmes, clients often now have the opportunity to experience a virtual building before the actual building is tendered.

Architects' training

Architects undergo five years of university education (an honours degree and two years of postgraduate study), plus two years of practical training before they are eligible to take their final professional exams. The title 'architect' is protected by law in the UK by the Architects Act 1997, so that only those who have undergone this rigorous training and are registered with the Architects Registration Board (ARB) are entitled to use it. Watch out for companies styling themselves as 'architectural' designers or similar wording, because this is generally an indication that they are not eligible. Only architects registered with the ARB are eligible to become members of the Royal Institute of British Architects (RIBA).

The five-year university training teaches architects how to interpret a brief and develop a range of design options that meet it, working with their client to find the one that best suits their aspirations. It also teaches thinking creatively 'outside the box' and developing the conceptual ideas into technical drawings and specifications to enable a building contractor to price and then construct the building. Architects also learn about the complicated town planning process; achieving a 'good' planning permission is an area where architects excel, often raising the value of the land by a multiple of their fee.

Architects apply impartial and creative thinking to projects large and small, whether you are constructing, adapting or expanding a building. They will guide you through the design, planning and construction process – from the early stage scenario of 'What do I do?' through to completion of the project.

Royal Institute of British Architects

The RIBA was established in 1834 and was granted its Royal Charter in 1837. It has 40,000 members worldwide and continues to perform its core remit of 'promoting and facilitating the acquirement of the knowledge of the various arts and sciences connected therewith'. The RIBA is a mark of quality. Architects who are members of the RIBA can call on a range of resources to broaden their knowledge that are not available to non-members.

Architectural practices can apply to become a RIBA Chartered Practice (see Chapter 9).

All RIBA Chartered Practices must have at least one of the principals and one in 10 of the employees in the firm being RIBA Chartered Members, and all project work must be supervised by a RIBA Chartered Member. Clients who have used a RIBA Chartered Practice will receive support from the RIBA should there be any disputes.

All architects comply with rigorous codes of conduct set by the ARB and the RIBA. This is covered in Chapter 10.

Insurance

All architects must be covered by a proportionate level of professional indemnity (PI) insurance that can be called on should it be required. This cover must be maintained for the duration of the liability period after completion – either six or twelve years, depending on the terms of their appointment.

What services can an architect provide?

Your architect can provide a range of services including:

— Investigating the feasibility of the requirements
— Developing design proposals
— Applying for statutory approvals
— Preparing construction information
— Obtaining tenders for building work
— Administering the building contract.

An architect works with a broad palette of skills and can provide or arrange other services connected with the project such as interior design, landscaping or making measured surveys of a site or building.

For more details on what architects do, see Chapter 6: Project process.

02 SELECTING AN ARCHITECT

Paul Morrell, for three years the UK Government's Chief Construction Adviser

"

Architects are highly skilled and professionally trained to turn your aspirations into reality. They apply impartial and creative thinking to projects large and small, whether you are constructing, adapting or expanding a building. "

Before contacting an architect, you will need to draw up the project brief. Focus on what you want to achieve, noting down all your requirements and highlighting any problems that need solving. Think in terms of how you will use the space now and in the future, rather than what needs to be built.

You should then draw up a shortlist of practices. The RIBA can provide assistance on this (see Chapter 11: Find an Architect and Chapter 12: RIBA Competitions).

Contact each practice on your shortlist, describe your project and ask if they are available to accommodate it. If so, request literature that outlines the firm's qualifications and experience. Ask to see a portfolio of work, or to visit finished buildings, and visit their websites. Above all, talk to your intended architect. It is important to ensure that you are compatible. Your architects must convince you both of their creativity and their ability to get things done.

What to ask for

You may ask the architect to provide some or all of the following, in addition to the proposed fees, schedule of services and so on:

— Previous examples of similar projects
— The team to undertake the project, including relevant CVs
— A method statement as to how the work will be undertaken
— Company policies on, for example, health and safety, quality control, sustainability, equal opportunities
— Qualifications held and awards won
— Confirmation of professional indemnity (PI) insurance and public and employer's liability insurance.

RIBA Client Services	The RIBA Client Services team can provide information and help you with your selection process free of charge. They can be contacted on 020 7307 3700, or **clientservices@riba.org**. You can also make use of the RIBA Find an Architect online directory where you can create your own shortlist from over 3,000 RIBA Chartered Practices and 40,000 projects. Go to **www.architecture.com**. Alternatively, you can speak to RIBA Client Services directly and they will create a tailored shortlist of practices with the appropriate skills and experience on your behalf. The service is confidential and provided free of charge. *See Chapter 11 for further information on this.*

RIBA Competitions

An architectural competition or competitive interview can be a successful procurement model that helps you to select a design team or design. Competitions can help to drive up quality, stimulate creativity and innovation and generate a range of ideas to improve choice. The RIBA's dedicated Competitions Team provides a bespoke competition management service that is fair, transparent and well-structured, with a proven track record of success.

For more information on this service see Chapter 12.

A good working relationship between architect and client is crucial to the success of any project. You and your architect should discuss and agree on the scope and cost of architectural services before the project begins and ensure that the agreement is in writing.

The RIBA publishes the Concise Professional Services Contract, which is suitable on a project with simple contract terms where the client is acting for business or commercial purposes.

For clients who are looking at larger building projects, the RIBA publishes the Standard Professional Services Contract, which is suitable for any professional commission or project where detailed contract terms are necessary. It can apply to most procurement methods, including design and build (D&B). There is also a multidisciplinary services version for use where the architect is providing engineering and other services as well, and a subconsultancy form.

For more information on appointments see Chapter 4.

03

HOW DO ARCHITECTS CHARGE THEIR FEES AND HOW MUCH ARE THEY?

Public sector
education client

"

The architect [was able to] creatively transform [our] aspirations ... into a realisable and deliverable project. "

Architects' fees will vary depending on the location and complexity of the project and the level of service. Some architects will charge you on the basis of a total project cost, others on a fixed-price lump sum or on a time-charge basis.

Architects will generally determine their fee proposal on the basis of an assessment of the anticipated cost of undertaking the work plus a level of profit. Your decision as to which architect to appoint should not be based on price alone, but should be an assessment of the value they will bring through the quality of their work and their skill and experience as a practitioner.

On receipt of an enquiry from a client, the architect will first need to decide whether, in principle, they wish to undertake the commission. In doing this they will be considering such matters as:

— Is the project likely to proceed?
— Does this project fit with the practice's established ambitions?
— If a competition, is it one the practice stands a reasonable chance of winning?
— Is the commission of a type in which the practice has expertise, or in which it wishes to gain expertise?
— Will the commission help enhance the practice's reputation?

— Can the practice make a reasonable return out of the commission?
— Does the practice have the necessary resources to perform the commission, or can it perform them in part and sublet other parts to those who are better equipped?

Having decided that the commission is one that the practice wishes to pursue, the architect will need to ensure that they understand as fully as possible what is required in order to make a full and well-considered proposal for undertaking the work. The sort of matters they will need to consider include:

— Do they understand the client and their interest in the project?
— Do they have sufficient information about the site and its context?
— Are the client's objectives clear in terms of building use, size, build cost, programme, sustainability, other consultants, procurement and other aspirations?
— Is the scope of services required clear?
— What are the anticipated terms and conditions of the appointment?

If they do not have the answers to these questions they will ask – and if you are not able to answer they will give you guidance.

Calculating fees and cash flow

Fee scales have been ruled as uncompetitive for some time now, so the RIBA is no longer able to publish such information, even indicatively.

In assessing their financial offer to the client, the architect will aim to reflect the value they will bring to the project. In a competitive situation they will look to understand what the client is seeking – is it simply the cheapest fee or will other factors weigh equally, or more heavily? Architects' proposals will be structured to emphasise those aspects they believe will find greatest favour with the client.

Architects will calculate fees taking into account a range of considerations including:

— The personnel likely to be engaged on the project and the projected time to be spent by them
— The cost to them of delivering the work and their target profit
— The services to be provided
— The proposed procurement method (that is, how the building contractor will be engaged)
— The proposed timescale for the project
— The added value they feel they can bring to the project.

Once estimated, the fee may be expressed in a number of different ways including:

— A percentage of the construction cost
— A lump sum for the entire project
— Calculated lump sums for each work stage (refer to Chapter 6: Project process for an explanation of the stages)
— Charges based on an hourly rate and a calculation of hours to be worked against these rates
— A combination of any of the above.

The fee proposal should set out a clear programme for the drawdown of fees throughout the life of the project. A monthly payment schedule establishes a regular invoicing routine for the benefit of both architect and client.

It is a requirement of both the ARB and RIBA codes of conduct that the architect ensures that they have adequate skills and resources to undertake the project which the client is proposing.

If the architect does not have sufficient resources to deliver the requirements of the project brief, they may consider subletting parts of the work to others with the necessary skills and resource. If this is the case, the architect is obliged to state clearly what services have been included in the fee proposal, together with a list of assumptions made and conditions of the offer.

The RIBA publishes standard forms of agreement which include schedules of design services and role specifications. The schedule of services describes typical services that may be performed depending on differing forms of procurement of the building work. (See Chapter 4 for further advice on appointing an architect and the standard forms available. See Chapter 6 for information on the standard form building contracts and for an explanation of the different options for building procurement.)

Areas of interface between different consultants need to be clearly defined and the architect may provide a matrix of services to be performed by each of the consultants, plus the client and contractor, with their offer.

There is a wide range of additional services the architect can be asked to provide including:

— Principal designer (under the CDM Regulations) (refer to Chapter 7 for an explanation of this important role)
— Interior designer
— Project manager
— Construction manager
— Information manager (for projects that will use building information modelling (BIM) processes)
— Access consultant
— Expert witness
— Party wall surveyor
— Planning consultant
— Surveyor.

All of the above require specialist knowledge and expertise and you should check that the architect, or a sub-consultant appointed by them, has the necessary skills, experience and professional indemnity (PI) insurance cover to perform these services.

Refer to Chapter 5: Other consultants for an explanation of the work typically carried out by other construction professionals you may need to engage.

04

APPOINTING AN ARCHITECT – AGREEING THE TERMS AND THE SCOPE OF WORK

Industrial sector developer

"

[The architects] communicated my vision and expectations in a very clear manner. "

Both the ARB and RIBA codes of professional conduct require architects to record the terms of their appointment before undertaking any work, and to have the necessary competence and resources. A written agreement is therefore essential: setting out what the architect will be doing, the timescale for the work and the fee and payment arrangements. The agreement should record the services to be provided, state the obligations of each party, identify the associated terms and conditions, and set out the fee basis and method of payment.

Individual architects are required to be registered with the ARB, and are subject to its code and to the disciplinary sanction of the ARB in relation to complaints of unacceptable professional conduct or serious professional incompetence.

As the client, you should write out what you hope to achieve through the project (the 'outcomes') and any specific briefing requirements, plus the total available budget and any key milestone dates (e.g. for determination of a planning application and/or for completion of the construction work).

The architect will use the information you provide to prepare a fee proposal and once this has been accepted the agreement can be written up. It is a requirement of the ARB and RIBA codes that the agreement is in writing.

In exceptional circumstances, for example where the commission is for a limited feasibility study only in the first instance, or the work forms part of a speculative or conditional bid, it may be acceptable to rely upon a bespoke letter contract to confirm the initial appointment. If you choose this route, your architect should send this letter to you at the earliest opportunity following receipt of instruction. The letter should set out the terms and conditions under which the commission will be performed, and should include:

— The name of the client
— The name(s) of those within the client body from whom the architect will accept instructions
— The site address
— An outline description of the project
— A description of the services to be provided by the architect
— Arrangements for any of the services that are to be subcontracted by the architect
— The date on which the provision of the services commenced or will commence
— Services that are to be provided by other consultants
— Confirmation that the architect will use their 'reasonable skill and care' to perform the services
— The quantum and basis of calculation of the fee to be paid for the services
— Any assumptions made in the calculation of the fees
— Any exclusions to the fees
— Arrangements for cash flow for payment of the fees
— Arrangements for payment of expenses and/or disbursements or, if they are to be included in the fee, any limitations on them (e.g. maximum numbers of prints included or maximum travel distance included)
— Amount of VAT chargeable
— The time for settlement of accounts correctly rendered and for payment of interest should this not happen
— Limit of liability and level of professional indemnity (PI) insurance to be provided by the architect
— Confirmation that the architect will retain copyright over their designs (granting a licence to the client for their use on the project)

— The terms and conditions that have been assumed to apply to the provision of services and used in the calculation of the fees, and those that will apply to any future services in connection with the project, such as are contained in the RIBA standard forms

— Confirmation that the letter confers no rights or obligations on any third parties

— Reference to the ARB code and disciplinary sanctions.

The architect will ask you to read it, make sure you understand the contents and then sign and return a copy of it.

RIBA Standard and Concise Professional Services Contracts

The RIBA produces two standard forms for appointment of an architect for commercial clients: the Standard Professional Services Contract and the Concise Professional Services Contract. Both are divided into four main parts:

— Contract details

— Schedule of services

— The Agreement

— Contract conditions.

Additional briefing documents may also form part of the contract, if they are listed in the contract details.

The contract is between you, the client (the person or organisation that wishes to commission the professional services) and the architect/consultant (the person or organisation performing the services).

There is also a Multidisciplinary Professional Services Contract for use where the architect undertakes a multi-role commission including engineering and other services.

When to use these contracts

The RIBA Standard Professional Services Contract provides comprehensive contract terms and is suitable where the architect/consultant undertakes a commission for architectural services on projects using a traditional, design and build or management contracting form of procurement.

The RIBA Concise Professional Services Contract is suitable for commissions for simple, non-complex, commercial projects of any value, in which the building works will be carried out using forms of building contract, such as the RIBA Concise Building Contract, the JCT Minor Works Building Contract or the JCT Intermediate Form of Building Contract.

The RIBA Concise Professional Services Contract is suitable for commissions procured on the basis of a traditional form of building contract where tendering occurs at the end of Stage 4 Technical Design. (Refer to Chapter 6: Project process for an explanation of the various stages of a project.) If the building contract is to be procured on other forms such as design and build or management types of contract, then the RIBA Standard Professional Services Contract would be more suitable.

Both the Standard and Concise Professional Services Contracts are devised as an agreement with a business client or a public authority, and are not suitable for non-commercial work undertaken for a consumer client, such as work done to the client's home. Business clients include charities, religious organisations and not-for-profit bodies.

Client's rights and obligations

As the client, you have various obligations under the contract. The main ones are:

— Advising the architect/consultant of the project requirements and of any subsequent changes required
— Providing the information which is necessary for the proper and timely performance of the services
— Giving decisions and approvals necessary for the performance of the services
— Paying the architect/consultant for the services performed
— Appointing or otherwise engaging other appointments required to perform work or services under separate agreements and requiring them to collaborate with the architect/consultant.

You also have rights under the contract. The most important is the right to suspend or terminate the architect/consultant's services.

Architect/consultant's rights and obligations

The architect/consultant has various obligations under the contract. The main ones are:

— Exercising reasonable skill, care and diligence in performing the services

— Performing the services with due regard to the client's brief

— Advising on progress in the performance of the services, of any information, decision or action required or of any issue that may materially affect the delivery, cost or quality of the project

— Collaborating with any other parties appointed or otherwise engaged by the client to perform work or services.

The architect/consultant also has rights under the contract. The most important are:

— The right to retain copyright in the drawings, data and documents produced in performing the services (the client is given a licence to copy and use the drawings, data and documents for purposes related to the construction of the project)

— The right to suspend or terminate performance of the services because of the client's failure to pay any fees or other amounts due.

Other standard forms

Other standard forms that may be considered for use can be found at **www.ribabookshops.com**. Your architect can advise you on this.

THE TOFFEE FACTORY

ARCHITECT: XSITE ARCHITECTURE

CLIENT: 1NG

COMPLETION: DECEMBER 2011

The Toffee Factory rejuvenates a badly dilapidated Victorian industrial building where the river Ouse meets the Tyne, close to Newcastle city centre. Abandoned for at least 20 years prior to this project, the building has been cleverly reused to make extraordinarily successful workspace for the digital and creative industries.

The client, 1NG, was a public sector-owned development vehicle whose objective was urban regeneration and job creation. 1NG identified the Toffee Factory site as strategically important, located as it is between the Newcastle quayside and the up-and-coming Ouseburn creative quarter. Refurbishing it would attract not only jobs, but also further investment to the area and establish a much-needed riverside connection to the city.

The key to success was a commercially viable design concept, duly delivered on budget and on time by Xsite Architecture. Procured through an OJEU process (OJEU is the *Official Journal of the European Union*), Xsite stood out from the crowd in two ways. Being based in the Ouseburn

quarter, they were intimately acquainted with its economic and social dynamics. Just as important, they had an excellent track record for designing precisely this kind of building.

Anthony Crabb was project manager in charge of selecting them. He explains: 'Actually what really convinced us was their enthusiasm, which turned out to be paramount in selling the project through design reviews and in securing further funding.'

Xsite involved 1NG fully in design decisions, solving problems as soon as the existing building threw them up. They even suggested adding an extra storey on the roof. Not only would this increase the net lettable area, it also gave the project a front door at the level of the bridge. Crabb again: 'that was a master stroke. It added real value for us and demonstrated a deep understanding of our needs.'

1NG handed the award-winning building over to the council on completion with the workspaces 90 per cent let. Beneficial economic ripples include new high-quality housing opposite, a significant pitstop on the coast-to-coast bicycle route called the Cycle Hub, and a reinvigorated connection along the river to the city. It's easy to see why Crabb (now with development company Arch) has carried on working with Xsite, with two further projects behind him and a third on its way.

05 ENGAGING OTHER CONSULTANTS

Other than the architect, you may need to appoint other consultants. Your architect can make recommendations or you can consult the relevant professional institutions. The usual consultants are listed below.

Quantity surveyor/cost consultant

The role of the quantity surveyor (QS) or cost consultant is broadly related to the financial management of the project. The QS will be responsible for preparing a cost plan for the design and this should be kept up to date to reflect the current design proposal as the design evolves.

It is critical that the cost of the design is managed proactively so that the design is not subsequently found to be unaffordable and subject to cost-cutting, or 'value engineering' as it is sometimes termed.

Early on in the project, the QS can prepare the financial appraisal for the feasibility report. They can also advise on procurement and tendering processes, on contract documentation, on cash-flow forecasting, financial reports and interim payments, and on the final account in the construction stage. The QS can analyse cost information on other similar projects, local levels of building costs and cost trends and so on, and can judge whether your budget is realistic and compatible with other stated requirements.

Titles such as 'cost consultant' are now frequently used in preference to quantity surveyor, reflecting the changed nature of the role to include managing the cost of the project rather than purely measuring it.

— **www.rics.org**

Structural engineer

The structural engineer advises on and prepares the structural design for the project, including the foundation design. They can advise the architect on local conditions relevant to the site, such as soil and geotechnical factors, roads, sewers, water supply and so on. They can identify hazards and hazardous substances, arrange for site, structural and drainage surveys, advise on alternative structural solutions, prepare design criteria and calculations, and advise on structural aspects of party walls, temporary structures and demolition work.

— **www.istructe.org**
— **www.ice.org.uk**

Mechanical and electrical building services engineer

The mechanical and electrical (M&E) engineers will advise on and prepare designs for the various service systems in the building. They will advise on climatic conditions, energy use and conservation, emission problems and so on, and will consult relevant authorities as necessary. Increasingly, they play a role in delivering environmentally sustainable solutions and undertaking sustainable design audits. From this point of view it is important that they are involved early in the design process, when key decisions on sustainability have to be made.

— **www.imeche.org**
— **www.cibse.org**

Principal designer

Refer to Chapter 7 for information on this important role.

Planning consultant

On projects in sensitive locations, in conservation areas and with work to listed buildings, it may be appropriate to appoint a specialist planning consultant. Your architect will be able to advise on this.

Interior designer

Many architects provide interior design services and see this as part of the offer, but you may wish to consider appointing a specialist interior designer for more unusual or bespoke interior design proposals.

Acoustician

Where sound attenuation or specialist acoustic design is required, you may need to appoint an acoustic consultant. Your architect will be able to advise you on this.

Fire engineer

Where a non-regulatory fire-engineered design solution is required, you may need to appoint a fire engineer. Your architect will be able to advise you on this.

Project manager

Some clients appoint project managers to represent them in the project team, but generally this is a role the architect can perform.

Party wall surveyor

Refer to Chapter 8.

Landscape architect

Where the project has an extensive landscaped element it may be appropriate to appoint a landscape architect either directly or through the architect as a subconsultant. Your architect will be able to advise you on this.

Surveyor

If a measured survey of an existing property is required, you will either need to appoint a surveyor or the architect may be able to undertake the work. For larger projects this is likely to be a specialist service. Your architect will be able to advise on this. It is likely that the survey will be required before design activities can commence.

Construction manager

A construction manager (CM) will manage the subcontractors in a construction management contract, including organising the tenders and administering their contracts. Critically, the CM is responsible for coordinating the interfaces between the subcontractors. This role can be undertaken by the client, or the architect may be able to perform the role.

Information manager

An information manager is a separate role within the design team on projects that use BIM, and this role is responsible for managing the common data environment (CDE) used for exchanging and coordinating digital project information. The information manager has no design responsibility, but the role can be undertaken by the architect or the contractor if they have the capability.

Access consultant

This is a specialist role with regard to disability access.

06

PROJECT PROCESS – KEY STAGES IN DEVELOPING THE BUILDING

Residential sector developer

"

Using an architect increased the regard for our business's approach to design quality. "

All projects go through more or less the same process: from the initial briefing; through development of the design; applying for planning permission where this is required; producing the technical drawings for Building Regulations and for construction purposes; tendering; and finally construction plus, where required, post-construction activities. In some circumstances tendering is carried out at an earlier stage and this is explained below.

The RIBA has developed a 'Plan of Work' which sets out these stages to a standard that is used by the whole UK construction industry. It was initially developed in 1963, but the latest version was published in 2013 with some fundamental changes.

The Plan of Work 2013 is set out on pages 32–33. Further information on the Plan of Work can be found at **www.ribaplanofwork.com**.

It has eight stages, numbered 0–7. The Plan notes activities that need to take place at each stage and these are set out below the stage headings. It is important to note that planning permission is not a stage, but rather an activity that usually takes place during Stage 3.

The RIBA Plan of Work 2013

Stage 0 – Strategic Definition

Stage 0 is the period of consideration of the requirements or needs that may (but may not) lead to a construction project. This is usually prior to engagement of any professional advice, although it may be appropriate to recruit the services of a RIBA Client Adviser. See Chapter 13: Client Advisers.

Stage 0 is where you, as the client, decide there may be a need for construction and consider the desired outcomes. It may be that they can be met without recourse to a building project, but where the case is clear, or where further consideration is required to determine the need, an architect should be engaged to undertake feasibility studies which take place in Stage 1.

It is during Stage 0 that you consider which architect to appoint, as well as other consultants where required. The architect can advise on the need for other consultants during Stage 1 if this is needed.

Refer to Chapter 2: Selecting an architect and Chapter 4: Appointing an architect, for further advice on selecting and appointing an architect.

It is important to write down the outcomes you want to achieve (the Strategic Brief) and issue these to the architect/s at the start of the engagement process. The brief will develop or may even change later on, but your initial thoughts are a critical starting point.

Under the RIBA Plan of Work the briefing process is set out in three parts: Stage 0 – Strategic Brief; Stage 1 – Initial Project Brief; Stage 2 – Final Project Brief. This is in recognition that the brief evolves and develops during the initial design phases.

Stage 0 is used to ensure that your business case and the Strategic Brief have been properly considered before the Initial Project Brief is developed. The Strategic Brief may involve a review of a number of sites or alternative options, such as extensions, refurbishment or new build. By asking the right questions, both you and your consultants, working in collaboration, can properly define the scope for a project before design activities commence.

The ultimate success of your project depends on the quality of your brief; that is, your ability to clearly describe to your architect the requirements and functions of your building, and proposed methods of operation and management. It is wise to ask your architect to assist you in preparing the next stage of the brief (the Initial Project Brief).

Your architect will need to know:

— Your aims – what outcomes you want to achieve
— Your reasons for embarking on the building project and what activities are intended for it
— Your budget (remember this needs to allow for fees, disbursements and VAT, as well as the actual cost of the building works)
— Who will be making the decisions about the designs, costs and day-to-day matters when the project is underway
— Your interest in environmentally sustainable design.

Stage 1 – Preparation and Brief

At the initial meetings, your architect will listen carefully to your intentions and help develop the brief alongside the design. Timings and budgets for your project will be defined at an early stage and only after you have approved initial sketches will the ideas be developed further. Stage 1 principally covers:

— Developing the Initial Project Brief and any related feasibility studies
— Assembling the project team and defining each party's roles and responsibilities and the information exchanges.

The preparation of the Initial Project Brief is the most important task undertaken during Stage 1. The time required to prepare it will depend on the complexity of the project. When preparing the Initial Project Brief, it is necessary to consider:

— The desired project outcomes
— The project's spatial requirements
— The site or context, by undertaking site appraisals and collating site information, including building surveys
— The budget.

The RIBA has developed a Briefing and Evaluation Toolkit that can be employed. Your architect will be able to advise you on its use.

A project risk assessment should be prepared to determine the risks to each party. The development of the procurement strategy, project programme and, in some instances, a (town) planning strategy are all part of this early risk analysis.

It is important that the project team is properly established and structured, and lines of communication agreed, before Stage 2 starts in earnest.

Stage 2 – Concept Design

During Stage 2, the architect and the other designers will produce the initial concept design in line with the requirements of the Initial Project Brief.

It is essential to revisit the brief during this stage and it should be updated and issued as the Final Project Brief at the end of Stage 2. In parallel with design activity, a number of other related tasks need to be progressed in response to the emerging design, including a review of the cost information, the development of a construction strategy, a maintenance and operational strategy, and a health and safety strategy. An explanation of these can be found at **www.ribaplanofwork.com**.

At the end of Stage 2 the brief should be fixed and any changes should follow a 'change control process' to manage any potential cost and programme implications.

Stage 3 – Developed Design

During this stage the design is progressed until the spatial coordination exercises have been completed.

By the end of Stage 3, the architectural, building services and structural engineering designs will have been developed and coordinated, and the cost information aligned to the project budget.

Once you have approved the design proposals your architect will submit them for planning approval, if required. This usually occurs during Stage 3, but can be submitted during Stage 2. Bringing the planning application forward can have risk and the architect will be able to explain the relative merits of submitting the application at different stages in the design process.

Stage 4 – Technical Design

In this stage, the architectural, building services and structural engineering designs are now further refined to provide technical definition of the project and the design work of any specialist subcontractors is developed and concluded.

The architect, and any other consultants, will prepare the technical drawings and specification/s and/or a schedule of works that will be used for tendering and for construction of the building. The architect can invite and appraise tenders from building contractors. Tendering can take place earlier in the design process. There are broadly three methods of procuring buildings:

1. Traditional
2. Design and build
3. Construction management.

Your architect will be able to advise on the most appropriate form of procurement, but a brief description of each is given in the box opposite.

It is broadly accepted that of the three measures of project success – quality, cost and programme – any one form of procurement will deliver two of these but not all three in equal measure. So 'traditional' forms of procurement will deliver better quality and cost control but will take longer. D&B will bring cost and programme certainty but at the expense of quality; and 'managed' forms of procurement will bring quality and programme benefits but will bring less certainty of cost control.

The three options for building procurement

Traditional

In traditional procurement, the design is fully detailed before seeking tenders. In this way, the contractor is pricing a full set of information and cost and quality can be controlled. However, it comes at the price of taking longer overall. The quality depends on having a comprehensive set of technical drawings and specifications at tender stage.

Design and build

In D&B, the contractor prices the job at an earlier stage and usually before a full set of technical drawings have been produced (i.e. before the end of Stage 4 and sometimes during Stage 3). The contractor will then be responsible for developing the final technical design. The contractor also fixes their price, and so this form of procurement brings programme benefits and cost certainty. However, it can be at the expense of quality because it is often the case that the details and specification, which are not fully developed at that stage, are altered for the contractor's economic advantage, while still technically complying with the tender information.

The architect can be 'novated' to the contractor to complete the technical design information, if that is desired by the client/employer. (Note that this should be written into the architect's appointment at the outset.) Alternatively, the architect can remain 'client side' and act as the employer's agent to oversee the work of the contractor and monitor the progress and quality of the work. The architect can do both, but in such circumstances there must be a clear contractual and administrative separation of the two functions. Your architect will be able to explain this in more detail if necessary.

Construction management

In managed procurement, a consultant or the client themselves acts as main contractor but subcontracts the various 'trades' (e.g. foundations, external walls and roof, plumbing). This form of procurement has time and quality benefits, but needs skilled leadership to manage the interfaces between the 'packages' and to control cost.

Choice of procurement route is an important consideration that will have a significant effect on the outcome of your project, and your architect will be able to advise on the best solution for your particular situation.

By the end of Stage 4 all aspects of the design will be completed, apart from minor queries arising from the site during the construction stage. In many projects, Stage 4 and 5 work occurs concurrently, particularly any specialist subcontractor design.

It is recommended that the RIBA Concise Building Contract is used for all types of simple commercial building work. For more complicated work the RIBA Standard Building Contract should be used. These contracts, and the others that are available, can be purchased from **www.ribabookshops.com**. Your architect will be able to advise which is the most appropriate for your project.

Stage 5 – Construction

During this stage, the building is constructed on site.

Under a traditional form of procurement, the architect can administer the building contract, carry out regular inspections, deal with queries, instruct any additional work required, monitor progress on site, keep track of cost, value the works and certify payments due to the builder.

It is important to understand that the building contract is between you – the client – and the builder/contractor. The architect can administer the contract on your behalf but is not a party to it.

When the project is ready to hand over, the architect – if they have been appointed as contract administrator – will inspect the building and issue a certificate of Practical Completion once the works have been finished in accordance with the contract documents. This is the final activity in Stage 5.

Insurance

It is very important that you have the necessary insurance cover to any existing building before construction work begins. Speak to your buildings insurance provider and tell them what work is being undertaken and the anticipated duration. Remember to notify the insurer when the work has been completed.

Make sure also that the contractor takes out insurance to cover the works and against injury to third parties. This should include:

— Public liability insurance to cover injury to a third party (such as a passing pedestrian) and damage to third-party property
— Employer's liability insurance, which is a legal requirement for limited companies and covers injury to employees
— Contractors' all-risk cover (which many builders do not bother with), which covers accidental damage to work carried out by the builder before completion or before the homeowner's policy has been extended to cover it.

Note that if the contractor is undertaking design activities they should also have professional indemnity (PI) insurance.

Stage 6 – Handover and Close Out

The project team's priorities during this stage will be facilitating the successful handover of the building. If the architect is the contract administrator, they will also certify the final payment, usually six or 12 months after Practical Completion following the defects fixing period. This is a period allowed for any defects or shrinkages to be picked up, following which the contractor will return to site to make good. A small amount of the contract sum is held back ('retention') until this has been carried out.

Stage 7 – In Use

Stage 7 is the building in use and is not generally a stage where there is specific work undertaken by the architect. The exception is where some form of post-occupancy evaluation is undertaken, for example to assess the energy efficiency of the building. This sort of exercise is more typical of larger developments for clients where lessons can be learned for future developments. If such exercises are to be undertaken, they would usually be under a separate appointment.

RIBA ⬛

The **RIBA Plan of Work 2013** organises the process of briefing, designing, constructing, maintaining, operating and using building projects into a number of key stages. The content of stages may vary or overlap to suit specific project requirements.

RIBA Plan of Work 2013

Stages ➤

Tasks ⬇	**0** Strategic Definition	**1** Preparation and Brief	**2** Concept Design	**3** Developed Design
Core Objectives	Identify client's **Business Case** and **Strategic Brief** and other core project requirements.	Develop **Project Objectives**, including **Quality Objectives** and **Project Outcomes**, **Sustainability Aspirations**, **Project Budget**, other parameters or constraints and develop **Initial Project Brief**. Undertake **Feasibility Studies** and review of **Site Information**.	Prepare **Concept Design**, including outline proposals for structural design, building services systems, outline specifications and preliminary **Cost Information** along with relevant **Project Strategies** in accordance with **Design Programme**. Agree alterations to brief and issue **Final Project Brief**.	Prepare **Developed Design**, including coordinated and updated proposals for structural design, building services systems, outline specifications, **Cost Information** and **Project Strategies** in accordance with **Design Programme**.
Procurement *Variable task bar	Initial considerations for assembling the project team.	Prepare **Project Roles Table** and **Contractual Tree** and continue assembling the project team.	← The procurement strategy does not fundamentally alter the progression of the design or the level of detail prepared at	a given stage. However, **Information Exchanges** will vary depending on the selected procurement route and **Building Contract**. A bespoke **RIBA Plan of Work**
Programme *Variable task bar	Establish **Project Programme**.	Review **Project Programme**.	Review **Project Programme**.	← The procurement route may dictate the **Project Programme** and result in certain stages overlapping
(Town) Planning *Variable task bar	Pre-application discussions.	Pre-application discussions.	← Planning applications are typically made using the Stage 3 output.	A bespoke **RIBA Plan of Work 2013** will identify when the
Suggested Key Support Tasks	Review **Feedback** from previous projects.	Prepare **Handover Strategy** and **Risk Assessments**. Agree **Schedule of Services**, **Design Responsibility Matrix** and **Information Exchanges** and prepare **Project Execution Plan** including **Technology** and **Communication Strategies** and consideration of **Common Standards** to be used.	Prepare **Sustainability Strategy, Maintenance and Operational Strategy** and review **Handover Strategy** and **Risk Assessments**. Undertake third party consultations as required and any **Research and Development** aspects. Review and update **Project Execution Plan**. Consider **Construction Strategy**, including offsite fabrication, and develop **Health and Safety Strategy**.	Review and update **Sustainability, Maintenance and Operational** and **Handover Strategies** and **Risk Assessments**. Undertake third party consultations as required and conclude **Research and Development** aspects. Review and update **Project Execution Plan**, including **Change Control Procedures**. Review and update **Construction** and **Health and Safety Strategies**.
Sustainability Checkpoints	Sustainability Checkpoint — 0	Sustainability Checkpoint — 1	Sustainability Checkpoint — 2	Sustainability Checkpoint — 3
Information Exchanges (at stage completion)	**Strategic Brief.**	**Initial Project Brief.**	**Concept Design** including outline structural and building services design, associated **Project Strategies**, preliminary **Cost Information** and **Final Project Brief**.	**Developed Design**, including the coordinated architectural, structural and building services design and updated **Cost Information**.
UK Government Information Exchanges	Not required.	Required.	Required.	Required.

*Variable task bar – in creating a bespoke project or practice specific RIBA Plan of Work 2013 via www.ribaplanofwork.com a specific bar is selected from a number of options.

The **RIBA Plan of Work 2013** should be used solely as guidance for the preparation of detailed professional services contracts and building contracts.

4 Technical Design	**5** Construction	**6** Handover and Close Out	**7** In Use
Prepare **Technical Design** in accordance with **Design Responsibility Matrix** and **Project Strategies** to include all architectural, structural and building services information, specialist subcontractor design and specifications, in accordance with **Design Programme**.	Offsite manufacturing and onsite **Construction** in accordance with **Construction Programme** and resolution of **Design Queries** from site as they arise.	Handover of building and conclusion of **Building Contract**.	Undertake **In Use** services in accordance with **Schedule of Services**.
2013 will set out the specific tendering and procurement activities that will occur at each stage in relation to the chosen procurement route.	Administration of **Building Contract**, including regular site inspections and review of progress.	Conclude administration of **Building Contract**.	
or being undertaken concurrently. A bespoke **RIBA Plan of Work 2013** will clarify the stage overlaps.	The **Project Programme** will set out the specific stage dates and detailed programme durations.		
planning application is to be made.			
Review and update **Sustainability, Maintenance and Operational** and **Handover Strategies** and **Risk Assessments**. Prepare and submit Building Regulations submission and any other third party submissions requiring consent. Review and update **Project Execution Plan**. Review **Construction Strategy**, including sequencing, and update **Health and Safety Strategy**.	Review and update **Sustainability Strategy** and implement **Handover Strategy**, including agreement of information required for commissioning, training, handover, asset management, future monitoring and maintenance and ongoing compilation of **'As-constructed' Information**. Update **Construction** and **Health and Safety Strategies**.	Carry out activities listed in **Handover Strategy** including **Feedback** for use during the future life of the building or on future projects. Updating of **Project Information** as required.	Conclude activities listed in **Handover Strategy** including **Post-occupancy Evaluation**, review of **Project Performance, Project Outcomes** and **Research and Development** aspects. Updating of **Project Information**, as required, in response to ongoing client **Feedback** until the end of the building's life.
Sustainability Checkpoint — 4	Sustainability Checkpoint — 5	Sustainability Checkpoint — 6	Sustainability Checkpoint — 7
Completed **Technical Design** of the project.	**'As-constructed' Information**.	Updated **'As-constructed' Information**.	**'As-constructed' Information** updated in response to ongoing client **Feedback** and maintenance or operational developments.
Not required.	Not required.	Required.	As required.

© RIBA

07 | CONSTRUCTION (DESIGN AND MANAGEMENT) REGULATIONS 2015

The Construction (Design and Management) Regulations 2015 (abbreviated to the CDM Regulations) are the regulations for managing the health, safety and welfare of construction projects.

The CDM Regulations place a duty on the client to make suitable arrangements for managing a project, including making sure that other duty holders are appointed (i.e. the principal designer and principal contractor) and that sufficient time and resources are allocated. Clients must also make sure that relevant information is prepared and provided to the other duty holders; that the principal designer and principal contractor carry out their duties; and that welfare facilities are provided.

Under the CDM Regulations, there are two key phases of a project: the preconstruction phase and the construction phase. Preconstruction includes all activities prior to construction, including design activities that take place after construction has commenced. Broadly speaking, the principal designer is responsible for managing the preconstruction phase and the principal contractor the construction phase.

It is important to note that where an appointment for principal designer has not been made in writing, the duties remain with the client.

The principal designer will usually be the architect, but should be the member of the design team most able to lead the design process and communicate with the other designers and the other duty holders under the CDM Regulations. The appointment should be separate to that as architect/designer, with a separate fee, and may have different terms and conditions and a different duration and scope. That is, it may last more or less time than the architect/designer's appointment.

Principal designers must have technical knowledge of the construction industry relevant to the project and the experience required to manage and coordinate the preconstruction phase. Principal designers are required to:

— Disseminate all relevant preexisting information on the project
— Plan, manage, monitor and coordinate health and safety during the preconstruction phase
— Ensure the design team works 'so far as reasonably practicable' to reduce risks, coordinate information, and generate solutions for construction, maintenance and cleaning that are as risk free as possible
— Ensure that relevant and proportionate preconstruction information regarding the project, both prior to the current work and as generated by the team, is handed over to the principal contractor and other designers and contractors
— Generate and organise proportionate information for the health and safety file and hand this over to the client at the end of their commission.

Client duties

The client must provide any information they already have on any existing building and the site as soon as possible. This would include surveys, the results of investigations, any existing health and safety file, and so on, that can help with design and planning of construction activities. The principal designer will assist in this activity and disseminate it to the other project team members, with existing hazards identified, as necessary.

You will also need to agree with the principal designer what information will be needed for the health and safety file, which is a record of all health and safety information needed during use, maintenance and ultimately demolition of the building.

It is the client's duty to notify the enforcing authorities where the project is expected to last longer than 30 working days and have more than 20 workers working on the site at any one time, or exceed 500 person days. This is called an 'F10 notification'.

Information on how to notify construction work can be found at
www.hse.gov.uk/construction/cdm/faq/notification.htm.

Your architect will be able to advise you on your duties. Refer also to
Industry Guidance for Clients, published by the HSE (**www.hse.gov.uk**).

The following checklist for clients has been published by the HSE:

	CDM Regulations checklist for clients	Tick
1	Are you clear about your responsibilities?	
2	Have you made your formal appointments?	
3	Have you checked that the principal designer or designer has the capability and necessary skills, knowledge, training and experience to fulfil their duties?	
4	Have you checked that the principal contractor or contractor has the capability and necessary skills, knowledge, training and experience to fulfil their duties?	
5	Have you checked that the project team is adequately resourced?	
6	Has a project or client brief been issued to the project team?	
7	Has the project team been provided with information about the existing site or structure (preconstruction information)?	
8	Do you have access to project-specific health and safety advice?	
9	Are suitable arrangements in place to manage health and safety throughout the project?	
10	Has a schedule of the key activities for the project been produced?	
11	Has sufficient time been allowed to complete the key activities?	

	CDM Regulations checklist for clients	Tick
12	Where required, has an online F10 notification form been submitted to HSE to notify them of commencement of work?	
13	Have you checked that a construction phase plan has been adequately developed before work starts on site?	
14	Are you satisfied that suitable welfare facilities have been provided before work starts on site?	
15	Have you agreed the format and content of the health and safety file?	

© CITB (2015) CDM 2015 Industry Guidance for Clients

The principal contractor is required to produce a 'construction phase plan' setting out how they will manage health and safety on site. Before the work starts on site you, as the client, need to satisfy yourself that an adequate plan has been prepared. The plan should be project-specific, take into account the preconstruction information provided, and its contents should be proportionate to the site risks.

Under the CDM Regulations, clients must:

— Ensure suitable welfare facilities are provided on site
— Ensure that the arrangements made for managing health and safety during construction are working successfully
— Take reasonable steps to ensure that the principal designer and the principal contractor are complying with their duties. This may be carried out through face-to-face progress meetings or via written updates. Routine monitoring of construction phase activities is not required.

At the end of the project, the client must ensure that the principal designer provides the health and safety file. On projects where the principal designer's role has finished before the end of the project, the principal contractor will have taken on responsibility for the file and for handing it over to the client.

08 RELEVANT LEGISLATION

Building Act 1984 and Building Regulations 2010

The Act and the Regulations apply to England and Wales and aim to secure standards regarding: health and safety for people in and around buildings; energy conservation; and the welfare and convenience of disabled people.

The Regulations apply to all new building work and impose duties covering design and construction of buildings, their services, fittings and equipment.

'Approved documents' set out the requirements and give practical and technical guidance on compliance with the Regulations. The approved documents are lettered A–R, and cover: structure, fire safety, site preparation, contaminants and resistance to moisture, toxic substances, sound transmission, ventilation, hygiene, drainage and waste disposal, heating appliances, protection from falling, conservation of fuel and power, access and facilities for disabled people, glazing, and electrical safety.

The local authority must be given notice before work commences. Building control inspectors will make independent checks on compliance and issue a final certificate on satisfactory completion.

There are two ways compliance with the Regulations is ensured: through local authority building control inspectors or approved inspectors – either of which the client is free to use. Approved inspectors are private sector companies or individuals authorised to provide a building control service. Your architect will be able to explain this in more detail.

CDM Regulations 2015

See Chapter 7.

Equality Act 2010

The Act replaced previous anti-discrimination laws with a single Act to make the law simpler and to remove inconsistencies. This makes the law easier for people to understand and comply with. The Act also strengthens protection in some situations and covers nine protected characteristics that cannot be used as a reason to treat people unfairly. Every person has one or more of the protected characteristics, so the Act protects everyone against unfair treatment. The protected characteristics are: age, disability, gender reassignment, marriage and civil partnership, pregnancy and maternity, race and religion or belief, sex and sexual orientation.

The Equality Act sets out the different ways in which it is unlawful to treat someone, such as direct and indirect discrimination, harassment, victimisation, and failing to make a reasonable adjustment for a disabled person.

The Act prohibits unfair treatment in the workplace, when providing goods, facilities and services, when exercising public functions and when buying or renting property.

European Services Directive

A key part of the European Services Directive relates to improving consumer confidence when conducting business anywhere in the European Union. It achieves this by setting some basic requirements – ensuring that customers have access to a minimum amount of information and to a complaints procedure. Certain information must be made available, including:

— The name, legal status and form, and address of the business
— If registered in a trade of other similar public register, the register's name and the registration number
— If carrying on a regulated profession, any professional body or similar institution with which the business is registered, the professional title and the country in which that title was granted
— If required to hold professional liability insurance or a guarantee, information about the cover and contact details of the insurer and territorial coverage.

Housing Grants, Construction and Regeneration Act 1996

This Act applies to most construction contracts that include client-architect professional services agreements.

It is important to note that a construction contract need not be in writing for the Act to apply and a dispute arising from an oral contract can be referred to adjudication.

RIBA building contracts include terms to comply with the Act's provisions, which primarily relate to payment procedures and resolution of disputes by adjudication.

Late Payment of Commercial Debts Regulations 2013

These Regulations entitle a business to claim from another business simple interest for late payment and for reasonable debt-recovery costs. The statutory rate of interest is 8% over the official dealing rate of the Bank of England (the base rate). Visit **www.payontime.co.uk** for information about the legislation and an interest calculator.

Note that it is for the supplier, for example the architect, to decide whether or not to use this statutory right. Alternatively, the parties (the client and architect, for example) may agree different terms, but the Act requires that any alternative must be a substantial remedy. The Regulations do not apply where the payee is a consumer.

Party Wall etc. Act 1996

A notice must be served by or on behalf of the building owner notifying the owner and occupiers of adjoining land if:

— A party wall is to be demolished, rebuilt, extended or repaired
— A new building is to be constructed near the boundary
— A new party fence is to be built
— A new wall is to be built up to the boundary line.

If the adjoining owner does not consent to the works a dispute will arise. The Act sets out a procedure for resolving such disputes.

A party wall is one that either stands astride the boundary of land belonging to two (or more) different owners, or stands wholly on one owner's land but is used by two (or more) owners to separate their buildings. There are specific requirements that owners of such walls must meet when alterations are to be made.

For an explanation of party wall conditions and useful standard letters that can be used to manage the regulations pertaining to party walls, download the government guidance from **www.gov.uk/party-wall-etc-act-1996-guidance**.

Your architect may be able to provide advice on party walls, but you may also need to appoint a party wall surveyor. If you are not sure whether the Party Wall etc. Act applies to the work that you are planning, you should seek professional advice from an organisation such as the Pyramus & Thisbe Club, whose website is **www.partywalls.org.uk**. The club is a not-for-profit body of professionals that can put you in contact with local members who are willing to provide general and informal advice about the Act, and can usually provide you with names of party wall surveyors in your area.

Town and Country Planning Act 1990

The purpose of the planning system is to regulate the use, siting and appearance of buildings, and to protect the environment and public amenity.

All developments require planning permission from the local planning authority except for certain development within strict criteria which may be covered by 'permitted development'. Internal or external alterations that would affect the character of a listed building of historical or architectural interest require two separate applications, one for listed building consent and one for planning permission. If the site is within a conservation area you will need conservation area consent as well.

THE AVENUE

ARCHITECT: **POLLARD THOMAS EDWARDS**

CLIENT: **HILL**

COMPLETION: **SEPTEMBER 2014**

The Avenue, a housing development in the market town of Saffron Walden, breathes new life into land previously owned by the adjacent Quaker Walden School.

Overcoming significant planning sensitivities, the resulting scheme has won a clutch of awards and is much loved by its residents and neighbours.

Hill's attitude to briefing is perhaps unusual among housebuilders. Unlike its larger pattern-book competitors, Hill invests in bespoke design. Within certain target tolerances, they give their architects a free hand to run with their own ideas. Design Director Nick Parkinson, himself an architect, describes it as the best way to get the most out of the site, but concedes that it needs continuous review against the updated development appraisal: 'That way, we can ensure the designs evolve to address all requirements throughout the process'.

Parkinson also believes, as far as practicable, in keeping the same architect on board from beginning to end. 'It's about ownership. We don't want their design vision to get lost during construction. Equally, we want to make sure that our pre-planning architects are actually thinking about buildability.'

Having worked with the architects Pollard Thomas Edwards (PTE) before, Hill knew them to be a reliable, safe pair of hands. Planning consent was secured with a sensitive approach to the conservation area, the mature landscape context, the presence of a listed water tower, and a wary local community. PTE carried out the consultation process, impressing Parkinson with their excellent presentation skills. 'They worked closely with all stakeholders, communicating a clear narrative which won people round.'

In the end, PTE designed concepts and working drawings for a relatively dense site of 57 private homes and 19 affordable homes. A retained avenue of mature lime trees provides access to a series of homes configured into pleasant, space-efficient courtyards. Parkinson again: 'They hit the goals of design quality and viability. More than that, by pushing the brief they improved our bottom line.'

For Parkinson, the architectural approach made a critical difference. Inevitable stresses along the way were handled constructively, and coming in slightly over the original budget was more than compensated by better returns.

09 | RIBA CHARTERED PRACTICES

Public sector
heritage client

"

The excellent layout and design has significantly helped to attract more customers to purchase goods from our museum shop. **"**

Only architectural practices that meet strict eligibility criteria can register as a RIBA Chartered Practice. They comply with strict criteria covering insurance, health and safety and quality management systems. They range from one-person offices to large, multinational firms operating worldwide. RIBA Chartered Practices are the only architectural practices endorsed and promoted by the RIBA. The requirements for RIBA Chartered Practice membership are as follows:

— At least one of the practice's full-time principals (director or partner) must be a RIBA Chartered Member and on the ARB register
— All of the practice's architectural work must be supervised by a RIBA Chartered Member who is on the ARB register
— At least one in eight of all staff employed in the practice must be on the ARB register, or an Associate Member of the RIBA or a CIAT member with RIBA Affiliate Membership
— At least one in 10 of all staff employed in the practice must be a RIBA Chartered Member or Associate Member
— The practice must have a current and appropriate professional indemnity (PI) insurance policy
— The practice must operate an appropriate quality management system
— The practice must operate an appropriate health and safety policy
— The practice must have a written employment policy in place which addresses the principles of the RIBA policy statement on employment
— The practice must have an appropriate equality, diversity and inclusion policy in place

- The practice must have an appropriate continuing professional development (CPD) framework in place
- The practice must operate an appropriate environmental management policy
- The practice must commit to paying at least the Living Wage (or London Living Wage, where appropriate) to architecture students working within the practice.

All practices registered with the RIBA Chartered Practice scheme and their staff are expected to conduct themselves in accordance with a code of practice and in a manner appropriate to their Chartered Practice status, and the practice will be liable to reprimand, suspension or expulsion if they do not.

The *Code of Practice for RIBA Chartered Practices* comprises three principles of professional conduct and practice – honesty/integrity, competence, and relationships – and the professional values that support those principles. A copy of the Code can be downloaded by searching 'RIBA chartered practice code' at **www.architecture.com**.

10 ARB AND RIBA CODES OF CONDUCT

All qualified architects must maintain membership of the Architect's Registration Board (ARB). Architects are expected to:

1. Be honest and act with integrity
2. Be competent
3. Promote your services honestly and responsibly
4. Manage your business competently
5. Consider the wider impact of your work
6. Carry out your work faithfully and conscientiously
7. Be trustworthy and look after your clients' money properly
8. Have appropriate insurance arrangements
9. Maintain the reputation of architects
10. Deal with disputes or complaints appropriately
11. Cooperate with regulatory requirements and Investigations
12. Have respect for others.

A copy of the ARB *Architects Code: Standards of Conduct and Practice* can be downloaded at **www.arb.org**

Architects who are members of the RIBA must abide by the RIBA Code of Conduct. The purpose of this Code is to promote professional good conduct and best practice. Members should at all times be guided by its spirit as well as its precise and express terms. Any member who contravenes the Code will be liable to reprimand, suspension or expulsion. (Chartered Practices must abide by the Code of Practice. Individual Members must abide by the Code of Professional Conduct. Both Codes have identical principles – Integrity, Competence and Relationships.)

Members must comply with all relevant legal obligations. It is not the remit of the Code to duplicate the provisions of business, employment, health and safety, environmental and discrimination law.

Members' conduct outside the practice of architecture will not normally fall within the remit of the Code and the institute's disciplinary procedures, unless the disciplinary committee determines that such conduct generally offends against the honour and integrity of the profession.

A judgment from a competent court or tribunal against a member in their professional capacity as an architect may be considered sufficient evidence of a breach of the Code.

Copies of the Code can be downloaded by searching 'RIBA Code of Conduct' at **www.architecture.com**.

11

RIBA FIND
AN ARCHITECT

**Dharmacharini
Maitrivajri**, London
Buddhist Centre

"

I am indebted to the architects for many things; their wholeheartedness for one. Each stage of the process has been characterised by their determination to do the best job possible and their commitment to a high level of architectural detail. The creativity and skill of the design team meant our imaginations of what was possible grew. **"**

The RIBA's online directory can help clients create a shortlist from over 3,000 RIBA Chartered Practices and 40,000 projects. Go to:

— **www.architecture.com**

Alternatively, the RIBA Client Services team will create a shortlist of Chartered Practices with the right skills and experience on your behalf. They only suggest accredited Chartered Practices, who meet the RIBA's standards of quality and service.

The service is confidential and provided free of charge.

The RIBA Client Services team can be reached at 020 7307 3700 or email **clientservices@riba.org**.

12

RIBA COMPETITIONS

Dr Maria Balshaw,
Director,
The Whitworth,
University of
Manchester and
Manchester City
Galleries

"

Since reopening, the Whitworth has attracted over half a million visitors, along with fantastic public and media feedback. It has since attracted 18 cultural, architectural and tourism awards and has been described as 'A beacon of elegance and intellectual sophistication'. The relationship between the building and its surrounding park is transformed physically, visually and conceptually and we've become a significantly more sustainable organisation through MUMA's rational decisions and commitment to deliver a 10% reduction in carbon output as set out in the brief. "

RIBA Competitions has extensive experience of delivering high-profile selection processes. Established for over 40 years, they manage competitions for a diverse range of project types and budgets on behalf of both public and private sector clients. They are widely recognised as the UK's leading provider of design competition management services, and can advise and arrange competitive selection processes to meet client's requirements. Using the RIBA to manage and support a competition brings credibility, prestige and rigour to the process.

With the RIBA brand you are sending a very clear signal to contestants that your competition will be efficient and fair, and that it will adhere to best practice standards. The RIBA can use multiple routes to promote your competition, including direct to its 40,000+ global membership.

Fees and a timetable are agreed with you at the outset so there are no hidden extras along the way.

For further information call 0113 203 1490, email **riba.competitions@riba.org** or go to **www.architecture.com**

What is a design competition?

Within the built environment, 'design competition' is the collective term for any process inviting architects and other related design professionals to compete against each other for a commission or prize. Design competitions can be suitable for a wide range of projects in the public and private sectors, such as:

— Urban planning and masterplanning
— New buildings and engineering structures
— Redevelopment and refurbishment works
— Landscape and public realm schemes.

The majority of competitions involve the submission and evaluation of project-specific design proposals. For publicly-funded projects, competitions must be organised to comply with public procurement legislation if the value of the project or subsequent commission is likely to exceed specified thresholds. Whether or not competitions are subject to public procurement legislation, there is still a need for a fair, properly scrutinised, well-managed process.

Why run a design competition?

The appointment of a design professional is the single most important task when undertaking a project in the built environment. Finding a suitable designer, even for a small private project, becomes a priority from an early stage. There are a number of ways of selecting a designer, such as personal recommendation, previous experience, research or existing framework. However, a competition based on evaluating the relative merits of several designers can give a client the best opportunity to make an informed selection. The competition system is the only recognised formal process which provides these specific benefits. A design competition offers many advantages, but may not always be appropriate (e.g. where a client already has a team with whom they have a trusted, established working relationship). However, a design competition can be a highly successful procurement model because it can help prioritise good design and bring the highest quality of thinking to a project. Competitions have a reputation for giving the best range of design options to choose from at a fraction of the total construction cost of a scheme. A competition can be used to select a design team including developers, a construction consortium or a design solution.

If you are unsure if a competition is right for your project then it is worth seeking further advice from RIBA Competitions. Mentoring advice is also available from previous clients on request.

13

RIBA
CLIENT ADVISERS

If you are undertaking a large or complex project the RIBA can put you in touch with an accredited RIBA Client Adviser, an experienced architect who can help define and prepare the brief, set up and lead the project team, draw up the business case and manage the procurement on your behalf.

On complex projects there are often a number of people who need to be involved in decision-making. Many organisations find it helpful to establish a committee to include all the people who need to be involved. However you structure your decision-making process, make sure that one person is designated as the point of contact between your organisation and the architect.

If you are thinking about appointing an RIBA Client Adviser you can contact RIBA Client Services on 020 7307 3700 or email **clientservices@riba.org**. For further advice go to **www.architecture.com/working-with-an-architect/client-adviser**

14 | MANAGING DISPUTES

Building projects are complicated, and despite the numerous checks and balances of the procedures and codes set out in this book, a dispute between the parties can sometimes arise. When this happens you need to have recourse to a means of managing the situation that minimises the impact on the project and the cost, and provides an appropriate resolution.

The RIBA Concise and Standard Professional Services Contracts (between you and the architect) and the RIBA Concise and Standard Building Contracts (between you and the contractor) provide mechanisms for this through mediation and adjudication.

It is helpful to know what the most typical reasons for disputes are and to ensure, as far as possible, that they don't arise in the first place.

The best means of avoiding disputes is to have open and clear dialogue: first in communicating the brief, then in having a written contract as well as written instructions to confirm any changes made during the course of the project, because these usually carry cost.

Common issues include 'what does the fee cover' and 'what stage has the project reached'. The RIBA Plan of Work can be used to clarify what stage the project is at and as a framework for the scope of work to be covered with regard to the services to be provided by the architect and other professionals.

The contract is key to managing the client–architect and client–builder relationship. The contract should set out the duties, responsibilities and scope of work in sufficient detail that there can be no misunderstanding about what is and is not to be done by each party. When filled in properly, the RIBA forms provide this detail.

The contract must set out clearly the basis of the fee and what is extra.

RIBA and ARB codes of conduct regarding complaints

Article 3.5 of the RIBA Code of Professional Conduct states that:

'Members are expected to have in place (or have access to) effective procedures for dealing promptly and appropriately with disputes or complaints.'

The RIBA Code of Professional Conduct Guidance Note 8 notes:

'Members are expected to have a written procedure which handles disputes and complaints promptly... The complaints procedure must be available on request to any complainant' (client or other stakeholder).

Standard 10.1 and 10.2 of the ARB Architects Code states:

10.1 [The architect is] expected to have a written procedure for the handling of complaints which will be in accordance with the Code and published guidance.

10.2 Complaints should be handled courteously and promptly at every stage, and as far as practicable in accordance with the following time scales:

a) an acknowledgment within 10 working days from the receipt of a complaint; and

b) a response addressing the issues raised in the initial letter of complaint within 30 working days from its receipt.

10.3 If appropriate, [the architect] should encourage alternative methods of dispute resolution, such as mediation or conciliation.

RIBA Chartered Practices

Where the architect is a RIBA Chartered Practice they must abide by the Code of Practice for Chartered Practices. Clients can make a complaint if a Chartered Practice, or a member of their staff, is in breach of the Code. The RIBA publishes guidance on this which can be downloaded from **www.architecture.com**.

15

CLIENT CHECKLIST OF ACTIONS WITH KEY MILESTONES AND WATCH POINTS

The following is set out under the RIBA Plan of Work project stages. For an explanation of these see Chapter 6: Project process.

Stage 0	Strategic Definition	Completed
	Prepare Strategic Project Brief. (Refer to Chapter 6).	
	Consider project programme and budget and the business case for the project.	
	Arrange any funding required.	
	Consider any project risks and make a note of them to pass on to the architect once appointed.	
	Agree a single point of contact to represent you as client to the project team, ie the architect, other consultants and, in due course, the contractor.	
	Review your client responsibilities under the CDM Regulations 2015. See table in Chapter 7.	
	Consider your position with regard to environmental sustainability and set this out in the brief.	
	Consider selection process and form of appointment to be used for contracting professional services. (Refer to Chapter 4).	
	Select and appoint architect/lead designer. (Refer to Chapter 4).	
	Select and appoint principal designer (under CDM Regulations). (Refer to Chapter 7). Note this is likely to be the architect/lead designer.	

	Collate any information you have on the existing site and building and issue it to the architect and/or principal designer once appointed. (Refer to Chapter 7).	
Stage 1	**Preparation and Brief**	
	With architect, prepare Initial Project Brief. (Refer to Chapter 6).	
	Agree target project programme.	
	Appoint other consultants as required. (This may take place in Stage 2 instead.) (Refer to Chapter 5).	
	Prepare cash flow/schedule of payments to be made through the project.	
	Review cost plan and project risk register and take any necessary action to bring these into line.	
	Agree project strategies for communication, town planning, procurement, building control and handover of the completed building.	
	Select the design option that is to be developed in Stage 2 Concept Design.	
Stage 2	**Concept Design**	
	With architect, prepare Final Project Brief. (Refer to Chapter 6).	
	Review cost plan, project programme and project risk register and take any necessary action to bring into line.	
	Determine whether party wall survey/award/s needed. (Refer to Chapter 8).	
	Approve the Concept Design to be developed in Stage 3 Detailed Design. (Refer to Chapter 6).	
	Agree a change control process with the architect/project lead.	

Stage 3	**Developed Design**	
	Review cost plan (or tenders as appropriate), project programme and project risk register and take any necessary action to bring into line.	
	Review and approve the design prior to submission for planning approval by the architect.	
Stage 4	**Technical Design**	
	With the contract administrator, review tenders and appoint a contractor. (Refer to Chapter 6).	
	Take out buildings insurance if required.	
Stage 5	**Construction**	
	Give possession of the site to the contractor.	
Stage 6	**Handover and Close Out**	
	Take possession of building.	
	Inform insurers that work is complete.	
Stage 7	**In Use**	
	Instruct post-occupancy evaluation if required.	

The following documents are available, free of charge:

— *Client conversations – Insights into successful project outcomes* (search online for 'RIBA client conversations')
— *RIBA Client Survey* (search 'client survey' at **www.architecture.com**)
— *Client and Architect* – developing the essential relationship (search 'client and architect' at **www.architecture.com**)
— *Need building work done? A short guide for clients on the Construction (Design and Management) Regulations 2015* (search title online).
— *Party Wall etc. Act 1996 Explanatory Booklet* (download free of charge by searching for 'party wall etc act 1996 explanatory booklet' at **www.gov.uk**)
— *CDM 2015 Industry Guidance for Clients* (download free of charge by searching for 'cdm guide for clients' at **www.citb.co.uk**).

See also:

— *BIM for Construction Clients* by Richard Saxon (NBS, February 2016) ISBN: 9781859466070
— *Being an Effective Construction Client: Working on Commercial and Public Projects* by Peter Ullathorne (RIBA Publishing, September 2015) ISBN: 9781859465769.

GLOSSARY

Architect

'Architect' is a legally protected title which can only be used by people registered under the Architects Act 1997.

Architects Registration Board (ARB)

In the UK a person cannot practise or carry on a business under any name, style or title containing the word 'architect' unless they are registered with the Architects Registration Board (ARB). The list of ARB registered architects can be checked on the ARB website **www.arb.org.uk**. (See Chapter 10: ARB and RIBA codes of conduct.)

Building information modelling (BIM)

Building information modelling (commonly known as 'BIM') is a process for creating and managing information on a construction project across the project lifecycle. One of the key outputs of this process is the building information model, the digital description of every aspect of the built asset. This model draws on information assembled collaboratively and updated at key stages of a project. Creating a digital building information model enables those who interact with the building to optimise their actions, resulting in a greater whole life value for the asset.

Principal contractor

Where there is more than one contractor (which is usually the case), one must be the principal contractor under the CDM Regulations 2015. The principal contractor may also take on the client's duties under the Regulations. See Chapter 7.

Principal designer

Where there will be a principal contractor there must be a principal designer under the CDM Regulations 2015. See Chapter 7.

Professional indemnity (PI) insurance

Architects must carry an appropriate amount of professional indemnity insurance. The minimum amount is £250,000 for very small practices, but the level of cover is contingent on the scale of projects the practice undertakes.

Royal Institute of British Architects (RIBA)

The Royal Institute of British Architects is a global membership body driving excellence in architecture. Founded in 1834 and awarded its Royal Charter in 1837, the RIBA is the UK charter body for architecture. The RIBA champions better buildings, communities and the environment through architecture and its members.

The RIBA also maintains a code of conduct and expects its members to work with integrity and honesty. In turn, architects will expect their clients to be honest with them and provide accurate information relating to the circumstances of their project, for example with regard to ownership rights and boundaries.

For further information visit the RIBA website **www.architecture.com**.

RIBA Chartered Architects

Architects practising in the UK who are registered with the ARB and are also Chartered Members of the RIBA are entitled to describe themselves as 'Chartered Architects' and to use the suffix RIBA after their name. A directory of all Chartered Members of the RIBA is provided on the RIBA website **www.architecture.com**.

RIBA Plan of Work 2013

The Plan of Work is a framework that sets out the chronological stages to a project from start to finish. See Chapter 6: Project process.